Materials

- **White butcher paper (background)**
- **Light blue fadeless paper (inside of globe)**
- **Black fadeless paper (silhouettes, globe, outline, and stand)**
- **Alphabet stencil (caption)**

Procedure

- **Cover bulletin board with white paper.**
- **Follow basic procedure for reproducing art. (See introduction.) Trace globe interior on blue paper. Trace everything else on black paper.**
- **Trace and cut out caption.**

Activities

- **Have a class discussion on the importance of protecting our environment today for the future.**
- **Ask students to write reports on what they can do individually to improve the world environment now and in the future. Have students illustrate posters on air pollution or water pollution.**

Materials

- Black fadeless paper (background, caption, and small silhouette)
- White butcher paper (large silhouette of graduate)

Procedure

- Cover bulletin board with black paper.
- Follow basic procedure for reproducing art. (See introduction.)
- Trace and cut out caption and small silhouette; attach to large white silhouette.

Activities

- List several unusual occupations on the board. Have students research these occupations and write about them. They should include what education is required for each career.
- Invite several local guests, each with a different occupation, to discuss their careers with your students, as a panel or individually. Provide students with a list of their names and occupations before the visit so that they can prepare questions to ask.

Materials

- White butcher paper (background)
- Red fadeless paper (stripes and caption)
- Blue fadeless paper (field behind the stars and caption)

Procedure

- Cover bulletin board with white paper.
- Follow basic procedure for reproducing art. (See introduction.) Add red stripes and blue field to the white background.
- Trace caption on red paper. Place same size of blue paper behind it and cut two sets at once. Use blue for shadow.

Activities

- Have each student design and illustrate a class flag. Display their flags around the classroom.
- Discuss the Pledge of Allegiance with your class. After this discussion, ask each student to write a classroom pledge.

ABCDEFGHIJKLMNOP2R
STUVWXYZabcdefghijklmnop
qrstuvwxyz 1234567890?!:;&$

ABCDEFGHIJKLMN.,
OPQRSTUVWXYZ!?

ABCDEFGHIJKLMNOPQR
STUVWXYZ?!?1234567890

ABCDEFGHIJKLMNOPQR
STUVWXYZabcdefghijkl
mnopqrstuvwxyz;!?1234
567890 ABCDEFGHIJKLMNO
PQRSTUVWXYZ.?!123456789

ABCDEFGHIJKLMNOPQRSTUVWX
YZ

Silhouette

Bulletin Boards for All Seasons

Bev Dana

DALE SEYMOUR PUBLICATIONS

*I dedicate this book to
my favorite silhouette,
my granddaughter
Dana*

Designed by: Bev Dana
Many of the illustrations were adapted from Dynamic Graphics, Inc.

DS11504
ISBN-0-86651-284-5

DALE
SEYMOUR
PUBLICATIONS
P.O. BOX 10888
PALO ALTO, CA 94303

cdefghi-PA-8932109

INTRODUCTION

Nothing stimulates the imagination quite like a beautiful silhouette! What is more intriguing than a mountain range silhouetted against a moonlit sky, or a city's skyline at dawn? Silhouettes only hint at what is actually there, leaving your creative imagination to fill in all the details. These intriguing possibilities were the inspiration to develop this silhouette bulletin-board book. The simplicity of design plus the sophisticated effect make most of these ideas adaptable for any grade level.

You will be able to reproduce these bulletin boards fast and easily by using an overhead projector and the transparencies found inside the front and back covers. While most of the designs are simple outline shapes, some contain a small amount of detail that will require a little more time and effort to reproduce. Older students could develop these bulletin boards for you. They will enjoy the experience of creating with an overhead projector and take great pride in seeing their "creations" displayed.

Basic Procedure for Reproducing Art

Simply follow these basic procedures for reproducing the bulletin-board ideas in this book:

- *Determine the bulletin board you wish to reproduce.*
- *Select the transparency with the appropriate art.*
- *Set up an overhead projector in an area where you have a wall or flat surface to draw on. (In some cases you may want to project and draw directly on the bulletin board.)*
- *Adjust to desired size and focus.*
- *Gather needed materials, which are listed under each bulletin-board illustration.*
- *Project art onto appropriate color of paper.*
- *Trace outline shape, add detail if indicated, cut out, and attach to covered bulletin board.*
- *Use white chalk for tracing on black or dark-colored paper. Chalk can also be used for adding detail, but materials will need to be sprayed with an affixative or laminated to eliminate smearing. (For sturdier art pieces, glue all cut-out pieces to manila tagboard, and then cut out the tagboard in the shape of entire character or object being reproduced.)*
- *If possible, laminate all art and captions so that they can be used from year to year.*

A Note on Color

We usually think of silhouettes as being black and white (black art on a white background or vice versa), but other colors can be used. Use your own imagination and creativity in determining color selections; however, in most cases black and white will present the most dramatic effect.

Your colors will remain vibrant and attention-catching if you use fadeless paper as stipulated in the lists of necessary materials. If this paper is not readily available it can be ordered. One source is Dale Seymour Publications.

Make Your Own Alphabet Stencils

On page 42 you will find a few sets of alphabet styles. You can easily reproduce them in the size you want by using an opaque projector or by making a transparency of the page and using an overhead projector. Trace them on tagboard, laminate if possible, cut out, and store for future use.

Author's Comment

I have tried to incorporate historical events and dates, famous people, and national observances into these ideas so that they serve as a teaching implement. On each bulletin-board idea page you will find suggestions for related activities.

I have thoroughly enjoyed developing this book and sincerely hope that you and your students enjoy this new approach to classroom bulletin boards. Any feedback would be greatly appreciated.

CONTENTS

Autumn

Winter

Spring Summer

Autumn

Materials

- White butcher paper (background and school house)
- Black fadeless paper (children and apple)
- Alphabet stencil (caption)

Procedure

- Cover bulletin board with white paper.
- Follow basic procedure for reproducing art. (See introduction.) (Red fadeless paper could be used for the apple instead of black.)
- Trace and cut out caption.

Activities

- Discuss classroom rules with students.
- Discuss with students the topics that will be covered during the school year. Mention anticipated field trips and special projects.
- Have students prepare one-page reports on what they hope to accomplish during the coming school year.

Materials

- White butcher paper (background)
- Black butcher paper (crayons and caption)
- Assorted scraps of colored fadeless paper (crayon tips and leaves)

Procedure

- Cover bulletin board with white paper.
- Follow basic procedure for reproducing art. (See introduction.)
- Trace crayon tips onto eleven different colors of scrap paper. Use three of these colors for leaves.

Activities

- Have students make two columns on an 8½″ × 11″ sheet of paper. In the first column they should list the eleven colors shown on the crayon tips. In the second column they should list one or two words describing what each color makes them think of.
- Show the students a color wheel. Discuss with them the three primary colors and how all other colors are formed from those three colors.
- Have students collect a variety of colored leaves and make a class album of leaves, identifying the tree each leaf came from.

Materials

- White butcher paper (background)
- Black butcher paper (football, outline, and character)
- Alphabet stencil (caption)

Procedure

- Cover bulletin board with white paper.
- Follow basic procedure for reproducing art. (See introduction.)
- Trace and cut out caption.

Activities

- Discuss topics and events to be covered during the coming school year.
- Have students suggest rules for classroom behavior.
- Discuss how sports are more than a game. Ask them what it means to be a good sport.

Materials

- White butcher paper (background)
- Black fadeless paper (key and caption)
- Alphabet stencil (caption)

Procedure

- Cover bulletin board with white paper.
- Follow basic procedure for reproducing art. (See introduction.)
- Trace and cut out caption.

Activities

- This is a great first-day-of-school bulletin board. Tell students this key belongs to them and it will open any door in the world, but it will only work once. Give them some time to think and then ask students to write about the door they want the key to open and why.
- Have students illustrate posters showing the doors their keys opened and what was behind them.

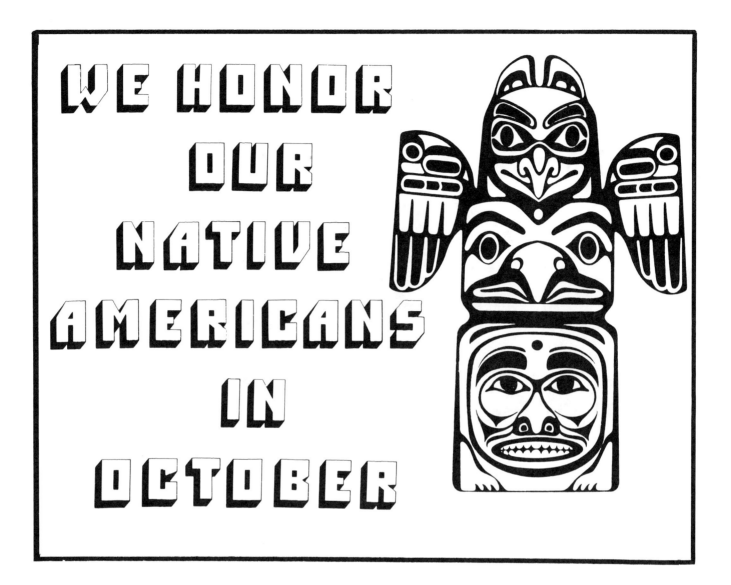

Materials

- Orange or yellow fadeless paper (background)
- Black and white butcher paper (totem poles and caption)
- Alphabet stencil (caption)

Procedure

- Cover bulletin board with orange or yellow paper.
- Follow basic procedure for reproducing art. (See introduction.)
- Trace caption on white paper. Place same size black paper underneath and cut out two sets of letters at the same time. Shadow white letters with black letters underneath as shown above.

Activities

- Divide entire class into five groups to represent regions where Indians lived: southeast, southwest, northeast, northwest, and the plains. Let each group work together in the classroom or school library to research their region's Native Americans. Have each group prepare and perform a skit for their classmates depicting traditions, activities, food, etc.
- Plan related art activities, such as layered-sand designs, that students can do that would teach them more about Native Americans.
- Have students design and color their own totem poles.

Materials

- White butcher paper (background and house)
- Black butcher paper (caption)
- Red, orange, and yellow paper scraps (flames)
- Wide black felt-tip marker (outline for house and flames)
- Alphabet stencil (caption)

Procedure

- Cover bulletin board with white paper.
- Follow basic procedure for reproducing art. (See introduction.) Trace flames on either the red, yellow, or orange paper. Place the other two colors behind and cut out three at the same time. Stagger them to achieve a color-variation shadow effect.
- Trace and cut out caption.

Activities

- Discuss with students fire hazards in general.
- Have students check their homes for potential fire hazards.
- Discuss safety measures to be taken in case of fire.

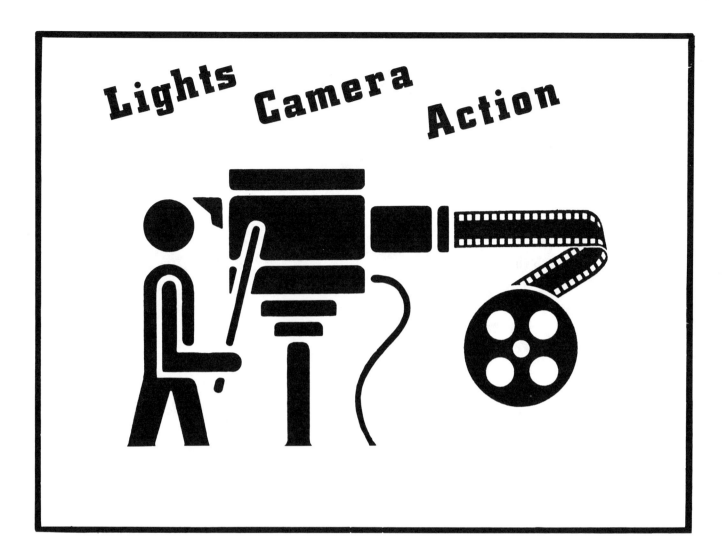

Materials

- White butcher paper (background)
- Black butcher paper (all art and caption)
- Alphabet stencil (caption)

Procedure

- Cover bulletin board with white paper.
- Follow basic procedure for reproducing art. (See introduction.)
- Trace and cut out caption.

Activities

- The first "talkie" movie was made in October of 1927. Ask students to research and find out the name of the movie and who starred in it.
- Have the class make a videotape movie. Determine first who will produce, direct, and star in the movie. Students should decide subject matter, set location, and name of movie. Students could have a premiere showing for another class when their movie is finished.

Materials
- Light blue or white fadeless paper (background)
- Black fadeless paper (bird and caption)

Procedure
- Cover bulletin board with light blue or white paper.
- Follow basic procedure for reproducing art. (See introduction.)

Activities
- Discuss the different types and styles of poetry.
- Provide students with a list of poets. From this list have students research and determine their favorite kind of poetry.
- Have students write and illustrate their own poems. (Haiku and cinquains are excellent types of poetry for illustrating.)

Materials

- White butcher paper (background)
- Black fadeless paper (tree and caption)
- Yellow fadeless paper (moon)
- Alphabet stencil (caption)

Procedure

- Cover bulletin board with white paper.
- Follow basic procedure for reproducing art. (See introduction.) Trace moon on yellow paper; cut out and attach to the board before adding tree and ghost.
- Trace and cut out caption.

Activities

- Have each student draw a ghost on large white construction paper and cut out. Provide students with several story starters with a "spooky" theme. They can use one of yours or make up their own to create their stories. They should write their stories neatly on the ghost they have drawn and cut out.
- Display their work on the bulletin board.

Materials

- White or light blue butcher paper (background and book)
- Black butcher paper (character and caption)
- Alphabet stencil (caption)

Procedure

- Cover bulletin board with white or light blue paper.
- Follow basic procedure for reproducing art. (See introduction.)
- Trace and cut out caption.

Activities

- Since the second full week of November is both National Children's Book Week and American Education Week, this would be the perfect time for a field trip to the nearest public library.
- Make a large graph on the bulletin board. Have students graph the amount of books read. Let students determine how their graph will be categorized and how the graph will be used.

Materials

- **White butcher paper (background and caption)**
- **Blue fadeless paper (caption and stars)**
- **Red fadeless paper (caption and stars)**
- **Alphabet stencil (for "November," "Is," and "Month")**

Procedure

- **Cover bulletin board with white paper.**
- **Follow basic procedure for reproducing art. (See introduction.) (Trace the word "Election" on the blue paper. Trace the ⭐ on red paper, leaving the large center star white.)**
- **Trace and cut remainder of the caption out of both white and red paper, using the red caption for a shadow. Cut extra stars out of both red and blue paper.**

Activities

- **Hold a fictitious presidential election in your classroom. Have students represent both parties and give campaign speeches, with the rest of the class voting for a candidate.**
- **Hold a class election for duties in the classroom. Be sure to have a ballot box and make the voting as official as possible.**

Materials

- White butcher paper (background)
- Black fadeless paper (radio and caption)
- Alphabet stencil (caption)

Procedure

- Cover bulletin board with white paper.
- Follow basic procedure for reproducing art. (See introduction.)
- Trace and cut out caption.

Activities

- The first commercial radio broadcast was on November 2, 1920. Have students research and find out where this first broadcast came from and what it was.
- Find an old radio script (available in playbooks) and have students simulate a "live" broadcast. They will need to do their own sound effects. Ask them to rehearse and then record their broadcast.
- Students could make up their own commercials to use during their broadcast.

Materials

- White butcher paper (background and cornucopia art outlines)
- Black fadeless paper (Pilgrim hat and caption)
- Alphabet stencil (caption)

Procedure

- Cover bulletin board with white paper.
- Follow basic procedure for reproducing art. (See introduction.) Trace the hat on black paper. Trace outline shapes on white paper. Cut out and place on hat.
- Trace and cut out caption.

Activities

- Have students recreate the first Thanksgiving by writing and presenting a play.
- Have each student plan a Thanksgiving dinner for eight to ten people. Tell them they cannot spend more than $25. As a class or individually, visit a local supermarket and do the imaginary shopping. Students should take pencils and papers along with them to write down the cost of the items they need for their dinners. Compare lists and see who was the most economical shopper.

Winter

Materials

- White butcher paper (background, stars, and center shape)
- Red and blue fadeless paper (stripes and background for stars)
- Red and blue thick yarn

Procedure

- Cover bulletin board with white paper.
- Follow basic procedure for reproducing art. (See introduction.) Cut a free-form shape out of white paper and trace caption onto it using either a blue or red wide felt-tip marker.
- Outline the board with the red and blue yarn.

Activities

- Since Congress officially recognized the Pledge of Allegiance in December 1945, this is a good time for students to do research on the background of the pledge.
- Have students recite the pledge and then list all of the words whose meaning they do not know. Using a dictionary, they should then define those words.
- Ask each student to create a new "Pledge of Allegiance."

Materials

- Black or dark blue fadeless paper (background, buildings, and caption)
- White butcher paper (snow, smoke, and moon)

Procedure

- Cover bulletin board with black or dark blue paper.
- Follow basic procedure for reproducing art. (See introduction.) (Only the white art needs to be reproduced and placed on the dark background. Use the overhead projector for proper placement of art.)
- Trace caption on the same color as the background and place it on the moon.

Activities

- Have students design posters or greeting cards using silhouette-style art.
- Discuss how holiday customs and observances vary in different parts of the world.

THE WRIGHT FLIGHT

DECEMBER 17, 1903

Materials

- **White or light blue fadeless paper (background)**
- **Black fadeless paper (airplane and caption)**
- **Alphabet stencil (caption)**

Procedure

- **Cover bulletin board with white or blue paper.**
- **Follow basic procedure for reproducing art. (See introduction.)**
- **Trace and cut out caption.**

Activities

- **December 17 is the anniversary of the Wright Brothers' famous flight over Kitty Hawk, North Carolina, in 1903. Ask students to write brief reports on Orville and Wilbur Wright and their famous first flight. Students could also illustrate their reports.**
- **Have students make a timeline showing aviation history up to today. This could be a class project.**
- **If possible, ask a pilot to visit your classroom and discuss modern aviation with your students.**

Materials
- **White butcher paper (background)**
- **Black fadeless paper (all art and caption)**
- **Alphabet stencil (caption)**

Procedure
- **Cover bulletin board with white paper.**
- **Follow basic procedure for reproducing art. (See introduction.)**
- **Trace and cut out caption.**

Activities
- **Ask each student to write five New Year's resolutions that pertain to the classroom. (They do not need to sign their names.) Collect the resolutions and read each one to the class. After a discussion, have students vote on the ones they think should be followed by everyone. Post the selected resolutions in the classroom for a constant visual reminder.**
- **Hold a classroom discussion on making and breaking habits. After the discussion, ask students to make lists of habits they would like to break.**

Materials

- Black or dark blue fadeless paper (background, rocket, and caption)
- White butcher paper (moon, stars, and smoke)

Procedure

- Cover bulletin board with black or dark blue paper.
- Follow basic procedure for reproducing art. (See introduction.) Cut stars, moon, and smoke out of white paper and attach to covered bulletin board. Then cut rocket and caption out of the black or dark blue paper and attach to moon.

Activities

- The first rocket was launched to the moon in January of 1959. Ask students to research and identify which country launched it.
- Have students plan an imaginary space flight to the moon. They should list all the materials they will need to take. Have them keep a daily log of their journey.
- Ask students to design and illustrate a rocket they would like to take them to the moon. Display their art work.

Materials

- White butcher paper (background)
- Black fadeless paper (silhouette and caption)
- Alphabet stencil (caption)

Procedure

- Cover bulletin board with white paper.
- Follow basic procedure for reproducing art. (See introduction.)
- Trace and cut out caption.

Activities

- Read Dr. Martin Luther King's speech "I Have a Dream" to your class.
- Have students research and write reports on how much of King's dream has come true since his assassination.
- Ask students to help you compile a list of famous black Americans and their contributions to humanity.

Materials

- White butcher paper (background)
- Black fadeless paper (star outlines and silhouettes)
- Alphabet stencil (caption)

Procedure

- Cover bulletin board with white paper.
- Follow basic procedure for reproducing art. (See introduction.)
- Trace and cut out caption.

Activities

- This is a great time to research all Presidents. Each student could select a different President and prepare an oral or written report.
- Have students write essays as if they were president for one day.
- Have students write letters to the President, explaining their concerns on world or domestic issues.

Materials

- White butcher paper (background and hand)
- Black fadeless paper (caption and hand)
- Red fadeless paper (the word "February" and heart)
- Alphabet stencil (caption)

Procedure

- Cover bulletin board with white paper.
- Follow basic procedure for reproducing art. (See introduction.)
- The star border is optional. (You may want to purchase self-adhesive stars in a stationery store.)

Activities

- Have a brotherhood essay contest either just in your classroom or inviting the entire student body to participate. School administrators, office personnel, and parents could serve as judges.
- Students could design and illustrate brotherhood posters for display throughout the school.

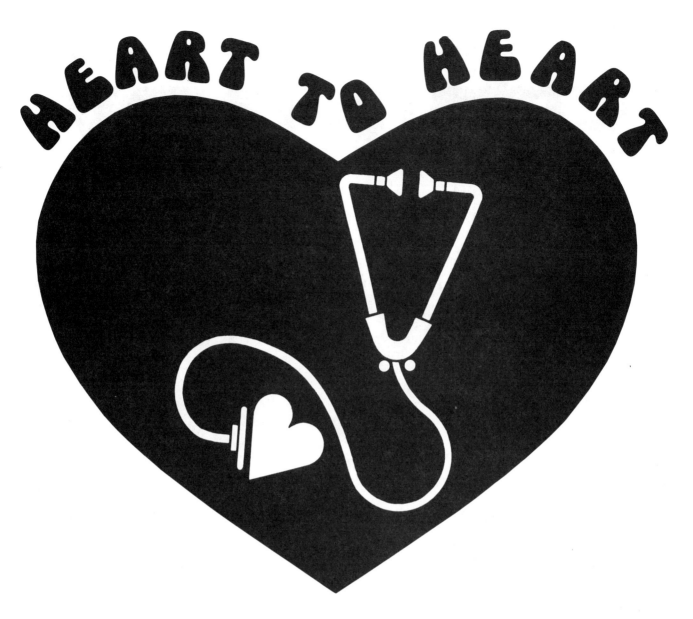

Materials

- White butcher paper (background, stethoscope, and small heart)
- Red fadeless paper (large heart and caption)
- Alphabet stencil (caption)

Procedure

- Cover bulletin board with white paper.
- Follow basic procedure for reproducing art. (See introduction.)
- Trace and cut out caption.

Activities

- February seems the appropriate month to discuss and research the functions of the heart.
- Invite a doctor, nurse, or paramedic to visit your classroom to talk to students about measures they can take to have and maintain a healthy heart.
- Have students write slogans, illustrate posters, or draw diagrams that deal with the importance and functions of a healthy heart.

Animal Silhouettes by Robin Angstadt

Materials

- White butcher paper (background)
- Black fadeless paper (animal, silhouettes, and caption)
- Alphabet stencil (caption)
- Thick black yarn

Procedure

- Cover bulletin board with white paper.
- Follow basic procedure for reproducing art. (See introduction.)
- Make zodiac outline with black yarn. (This can be done by projecting the shape onto your bulletin board and stapling yarn onto the board to form outline shape.) Trace animals on black paper, cut out, and attach to zodiac outline in proper sequence.

Activities

- Have students design a class mural of a dragon.
- Invite local residents, perhaps parents of students, who are of Chinese descent to visit your classroom and discuss the Chinese New Year's celebration as well as other Chinese customs and traditions.
- Plan a Chinese luncheon in the classroom. Select foods that can be easily prepared in the classroom. Invite the principal, office staff, and parents to attend.

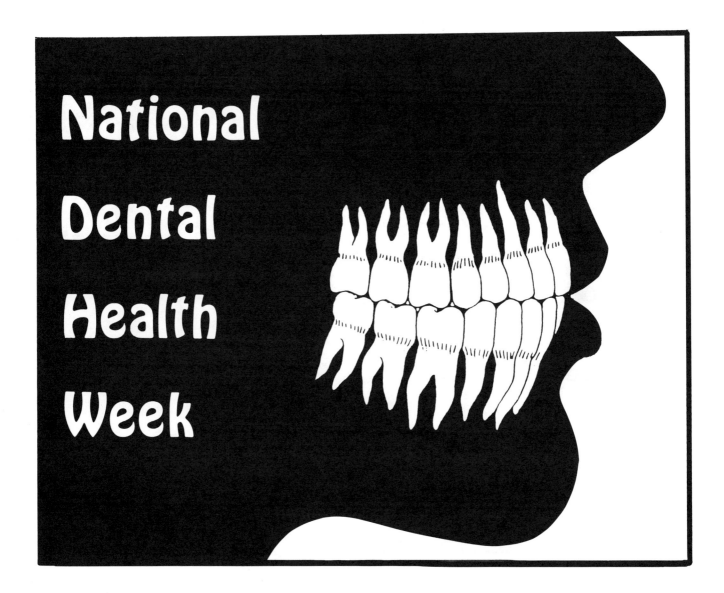

Materials

- White butcher paper (background and teeth)
- Black fadeless paper (silhouette)
- Alphabet stencil (if caption desired)

Procedure

- Cover bulletin board with white paper.
- Follow basic procedure for reproducing art. (See introduction.)

Activities

- The first full week of February is Children's National Dental Health Week. Invite a local dentist or hygienist to visit your classroom and talk to the students about dental health.
- Have students make collages or illustrate posters of foods they should eat to promote healthy teeth and gums.
- Ask students to prepare lists of foods that are harmful to the teeth.

Materials

- **White butcher paper (background and food)**
- **Black fadeless paper (plate, eating utensils, and caption)**
- **Alphabet stencil (caption)**

Procedure

- **Cover bulletin board with white paper (another light color such as yellow or pale blue could be substituted).**
- **Follow basic procedure for reproducing art. (See introduction.)**
- **Trace food on white paper and add to plate.**
- **Trace and cut out caption.**

Activities

- **Have students design posters or charts showing the four food groups.**
- **Prepare a graph that can be used for the entire class showing their daily intake from each food group.**
- **Have each student plan a breakfast, lunch, and dinner menu that meets all the daily food requirements.**

INTERNATIONAL WOMEN'S DAY IS MARCH 8

Materials

- White butcher paper (background)
- Black fadeless paper (faces and caption)
- Alphabet stencil (caption)

Procedure

- Cover bulletin board with white paper.
- Follow basic procedure for reproducing art. (See introduction.)
- Trace and cut out caption.

Activities

- List several famous women, living or dead, on the blackboard. Have students add to this list by using the library for research. Each student should choose one name from the list and prepare a written or oral report.
- Ask students to make their own lists of the major contributions women have made to society. Compile these lists into one class list. It would be interesting to make a timeline from the class list.

Materials
- White or yellow fadeless paper (background)
- Black fadeless paper (caption and art)

Procedure
- Cover bulletin board with white or yellow paper.
- Follow basic procedure for reproducing art and caption. (See introduction.)

Activities
- This bulletin board is perfect for displaying student art work. Put up some recent projects.
- If possible, plan a field trip to a local art gallery.
- Discuss different artists and their styles of art. (Check out art prints from your school library or a public library for this discussion.)
- Arrange to have a few local artists visit your classroom, one at a time or as a panel. Have them conduct a question-and-answer forum with the students. If you're lucky, they might be willing to present an art lesson.

Materials

- White or light blue fadeless paper (background and caption)
- Black fadeless paper (tree, deer, and grass)

Procedure

- Cover bulletin board with white paper.
- Follow basic procedure for reproducing art. (See introduction.)
- Trace caption on white paper, cut out, and attach to tree.

Activities

- National Wildlife Week is the third full week of March. Ask students to help you compile a list of endangered species. Write the list on the blackboard.
- Have students research and write reports on what can be done to protect our wildlife.

Materials

- White butcher paper (background)
- Black fadeless paper (all silhouettes)

Procedure

- Cover bulletin board with white paper.
- Follow basic procedure for reproducing art. (See introduction.)

Activities

- The first modern Olympic games opened in April of 1896. Have students research and write reports on why and where the Olympic games began.
- Have students make posters showing their favorite Olympic events.
- Provide a list of famous Olympic winners. Students could help you prepare this list. Ask them to write a report on their favorite Olympic stars.

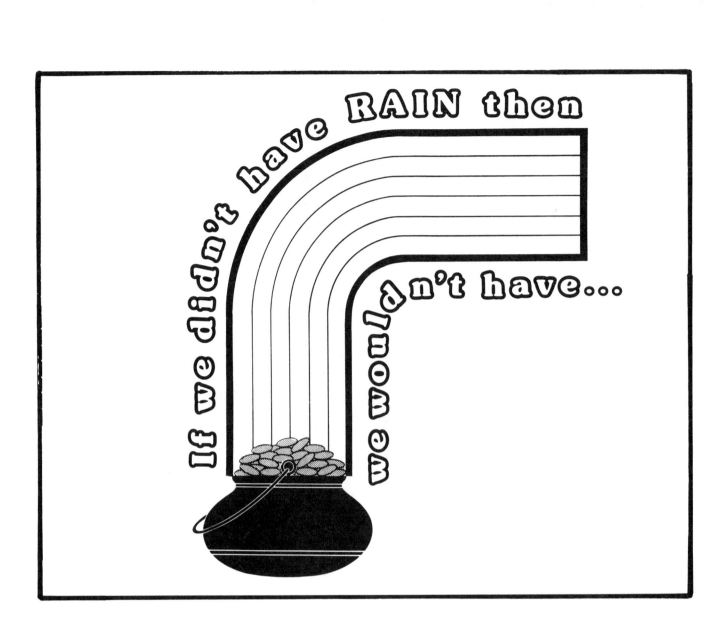

Materials

- White or light blue fadeless paper (background)
- Assorted colors of fadeless paper (rainbow)
- Gold paper (coins)
- Black fadeless paper (pot, caption, and rainbow outline)
- Alphabet stencil (caption)

Procedure

- Cover bulletin board with white or blue paper.
- Follow basic procedure for reproducing art. (See introduction.)
- Trace rainbow strips on the colored paper, cut out, and glue to a large piece of tagboard. Cut out tagboard in shape of rainbow.
- Trace and cut out caption.

Activities

- Have students make lists of all the things we wouldn't have if we didn't have rain.
- Ask students to write "rainy day" creative writing stories. (You might want to provide a list of story starters.)
- Have students design posters using the rainbow theme.

Materials

- White butcher paper (background)
- Black fadeless paper (ballerina, piano, and caption)
- Alphabet stencil (caption)

Procedure

- Cover bulletin board with white paper.
- Follow basic procedure for reproducing art. (See introduction.)
- Trace and cut out caption.

Activities

- Ask students to design posters announcing a talent show, a musical event, a play, or any school event that is upcoming.
- Plan a talent show in your classroom. Select students to be the organizers, announcers, and performers. Invite other classrooms to see their presentation.

Materials

- White butcher paper (inside of book)
- Black fadeless paper (all art and caption)

Procedure

- Cover bulletin board with white paper in the shape of the book.
- Follow basic procedure for reproducing art. (See introduction.)
- Attach caption and art to white book shape.

Activities

- William Shakespeare was born in April of 1564. This would be a good time to introduce students to his literature.
- Have students do monologues from Shakespeare's plays.
- Discuss with students how Shakespeare's literature is different from modern literature.
- Ask students to help you compile a list of authors of the classics. (They will need to use the library for their research.)

Materials

- White or pastel-colored fadeless paper (background)
- Black fadeless paper (clock and caption)
- Alphabet stencil (caption)

Procedure

- Cover bulletin board with white or pastel-colored paper.
- Follow basic procedure for reproducing art. (See introduction.)
- Trace and cut out caption.

Activities

- Since daylight savings time begins the last weekend in April, it is a good time to discuss spending classroom time wisely.
- Try to organize a day without clocks in your school. (The entire school will need to participate.) All clocks in the school will need to be covered for this day. Let the majority of students in each classroom rule on the time for recess, lunch, and other activities. (Teachers should have a watch, out of sight, for reference.) Discuss this event the next day with your students.
- Have students keep a chart of how they spend their time for one school day from the time they get up in the morning until they go to bed at night.

Materials

- White butcher paper (background)
- Black fadeless paper (silhouette and caption)
- Alphabet stencil (caption)

Procedure

- Cover bulletin board with white paper.
- Follow basic procedure for reproducing art. (See introduction.)
- Trace and cut out caption.

Activities

- Ask students to research why Cinco de Mayo is a day of celebration. After their research is completed, hold a classroom discussion on their findings.
- Plan a Cinco de Mayo celebration in your classroom. Ask parents or local residents of Mexican descent to help you with the preparations.
- Have students divide into groups of five or six each and make pinatas to hang in the classroom. (Perhaps they could each bring materials from home to put inside.)

Materials

- White butcher paper (background)
- Black butcher paper (carp and caption)
- Three colors of fadeless paper (carp shadows)
- Alphabet stencil (caption)

Procedure

- Cover bulletin board with white butcher paper.
- Follow basic procedure for reproducing art. (See introduction.)
- Trace front carp on black paper using white chalk for detail.
- Place the three sheets of colored paper behind the traced carp and cut all four out at the same time. Stagger the three colored carp silhouettes behind the traced one as shown above.
- Trace and cut out caption.

Activities

- Gather all the information you can on this special observance in Japan. Have it available for students to read and use for research.
- Have each student design his or her own three-dimensional carp. (Paper mache works well for this project.) After they are dry, they should be painted in bright colors. Hang the carp around the classroom for display.

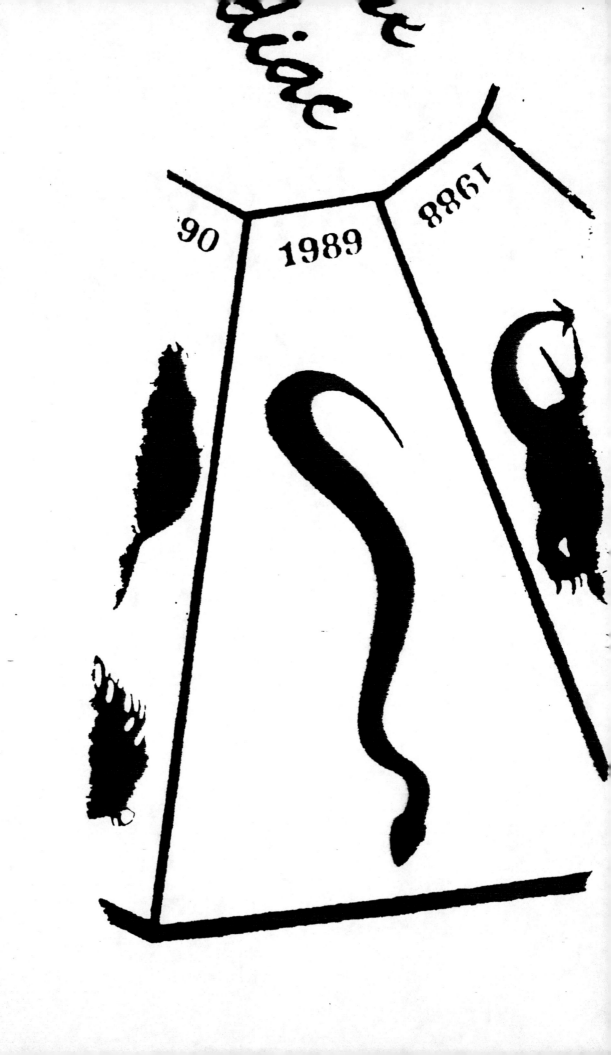